A Mother's Grief

BARBARA D. FLANNIGAN

HIS LOVE PRESS

A Mother's Grief
All Rights Reserved.
Copyright © 2019 Barbara D. Flannigan
v2.0

The opinions expressed in this manuscript are solely the opinions of the author and do not represent the opinions or thoughts of the publisher. The author has represented and warranted full ownership and/or legal right to publish all the materials in this book.

This book may not be reproduced, transmitted, or stored in whole or in part by any means, including graphic, electronic, or mechanical without the express written consent of the publisher except in the case of brief quotations embodied in critical articles and reviews.

HIS LOVE PRESS

ISBN: 978-0-578-22054-3

Cover Photo © 2019 Barbara D. Flannigan. All rights reserved - used with permission.

Outskirts Press and the "OP" logo are trademarks belonging to Outskirts Press, Inc.

PRINTED IN THE UNITED STATES OF AMERICA

An artist gave me this painting and I was so thrilled that Jesus saw Me so beautiful, and was in the Bible, Nephaniah 3:17 where it says He will rejoice over Me with gladness, and quiet Me with His love and with singing.

Table of Contents

Introduction i
Gratuitous iii
Part 1: Family 1
Part 2: Death 25
Part 3: Before & After 39
Part 4: Burial 42
Part 5: Trial & Penalties 49
Part 6: Hope 54

Introduction

This is a true story of my life, children, and some ancestry. The scriptures are from KJV version of the Bible.

There are times I grieve since the day the children died. So many whys? However, the Lord tells me to put the past behind me and I am seeking His face to accept and thank Him for what I cannot see, the future and trust Him for peace. Isaiah 43:18 says: Do not remember the former things nor consider the things of old.

So thankful for all the joy that You blessed us with, because your hand was upon us. He said we would do more than He would.

Gratuitous

Dear Bethany Greenleaf-Perez was the first person to add to the word Book and it came alive, for the Lord had mentioned book before I left to see her latter that day. She has walked me, by editing and encouraging with heart and her prayers. Janet Renfro, sweet sister, also prayed and gave me verses in the Bible and was beside me all the way and as you read my story, you'll see her throughout my life, thanks again. In our trials: thanks, goes to the Deputy Da for making sure everything went well in and out of court room, was excellent and stayed close to our conversations at break time. Honorable and courtesy and support even though it was out of town. Also, thanks to the Prosecutor, who recognized us with hugs and anything that was new or different for the new day. We will always remember these two- trial gentleman with love. Mostly I give thanks to the Son of God, Jesus Christ. When He told me in the middle of night, I would jump out of bed, run to the computer to write what He had told me, before I would forget it.

PART 1

Family

I WAS BORN in the city of Bowling Green, Kentucky on September 18, 1940 weighing ten pounds with no hair. I was the third child of thirteen children and one miscarriage. Eight children are still living. My Dad and Mother were Christians and many times we knelt on the floor while Mom prayed. As a child I loved to hear her pray. Dad was a epileptic sometimes having seizures 4-5 a day. Mom went to find a job but they served beer at this job so Dad said NO. Dad could not work and we were always hungry. Finally, we went on welfare. Grandma on both sides would help. Dad started having seizures when he was 14-15, and was kept at home. They could not tell anyone or he would have put in an asylum because seizures was from the devil. We were not to tell about either. I would listen in the morning to hear if he was nervous and going to have a seizure, not fearful if it happened or go back to sleep. Dad made a horrible scream when he had a spell, shaking trembling and foaming at the mouth. They were called Grand Mall. Then he went to sleep for about a half hour and was quiet for the remainder of the day. Dad loved us with all his heart. He told us ghost stories and wanted us to get a good education. He slapped me one time because I threw a Ponds bottle at him, dared him, so he followed through. If Dad was awakened in the night, he would always have a seizure.

SINFUL LIFE OF AN OLD MAN

I am too old said a withered old man
Soul
To change my way of life
The years of time have passed around
And left me here a shack.

I put off salvation when I was young
Because my days were sweet
The days went climbing into years'
That never can repeat.

Part 1

I often look into my life
    When my heart was tender sure
But now the bars are to my heart
    Leaving no door.

I'll just go trudging on my way
    On down the miry clay
For I have waited, it seems too long
    To ever change my way.

My steps are slow, my head is gray
    My eyes are dull and dim
But I can't look for any hope
    I have a life of sin.

My heart is hard, my days are few
    I can't be here very long
I turned away the love of God
    And lived my life alone.

Now if your heart is young and free
    Your steps are quick and strong
Give your heart to Jesus now
    Dear friend, don't wait too long.

Author: Mary Magdalene (Thomas) Craft

A Mother's Grief

My mother was never cited for anything. She was too busy surviving. Her dad died when she was twelve years old, and had bread and water for food. Her job was taking care of a male invalid for some money. Only she knows, what treatment was part of the job. I decided to add this amazing woman as a legacy to live on in the lives of her children after death. A compassionate and genuine spirit that had escaped me as a child.

When my mother went to the hospital to have my next to last brother, she wanted me to sleep with dad because I was a light sleeper and would wake if Dad was going to have a seizure. Sure enough, Dad was awakened by two nephews that was very drunk. Dad seized and fell on a bucket that had nails in side and hit his head. There was a lot of blood. He went to sleep after going back to bed. The Lord took care of him and I was so glad. There was no indication of injury. In the morning there was no more blood and all was well. Dad was not a complainer. He was a gentle and happy man. The only time he cried was when my younger sister had a seizure. He would be mean to himself for marring but never did talk about his seizures.

Mother on the other hand, would spank us always

Part I

with her hand, if we really needed it. Her patience came from Job. However, all the load of us children fell on to mom. When I was thirteen, I came in the kitchen behind the cook stove she asked what was wrong. I said I was sad and she said she thought the Lord was speaking to me. My dear Mother lead me to the Lord and I was Baptized. In 2015 I was baptized again, because I was in doubt if I really had been baptized. AfterI had left home, the Lord spoke to me how dishonorably I had talked to my mother in rebellion. I Called her and asked for her forgiveness.

My dad's mother bought a house for us before she died. No one could tell us to leave. It Leaked when rained, no indoor facilities, no running water, and no electricity. Most of our living would be from memories from January 1951. Mother burned the old house down in the sixties and mom and dad got a trailer. This is what I was told. But who could blame her? She had lost Her oldest child from epilepsy in a rain storm when he smothered. Perry had a paper route, and had seizure falling in mud on the side of the road. Also, there were rumors that he had been abused. After talking to my brother, Billy, (was 11 years old) he said that there was a rope ring around his neck and a rope was over the fence. We heard many cries in the night for many years. Mom had enough grief without looking at this broken down, house every day and no one's shoulder to cry on. Her only solace was her poems when she was overwhelmed. See my favorite poem below. She still had my brother's clothes in the upstairs from 1957, before she burned that old house down. I went with her to find him on the road. I was a sophomore in High School. The Lord says we never forget our children and she did not need any kind of memories. Isaiah 49:15 "Can a woman forget her nursing child and not have compassion on the son of her womb surely they may forget, yet I will not forget you." But I don't know of any way one can forget completely unless through death, or Alzheimer, which is what happened to my Mom. She did not know me the last time she saw me.

Mother had a near loss of another child, Sharon Kay, was born in February 1953. When she was born, her little body was blue but the Lord destined that she would live. They took her to the Hospital. She was a lady, quiet and smiley and a beauty. She was always okay, never complained about anything, always encouraged every one, quickly taking your side. She and I were the only kids to graduate from high school. She was the best of us. Her daughter, Michelle gave

Part I

me a story I want to share with you: Almost dark she got on a bicycle from an unknown and rode it. Then she veered off the road sustaining many injuries and cutting the ring finger off. Then lost consciousness.

Sharon loved her three children and five grandchildren; and lived for them. Six months before she went home to be with her precious Lord, Michelle and hubby took her into their home and carried for her. Their relationship was like akin to mom and child. Such great love.

When I got in high school, I joined 4-H, and we had a nightly program to bring our mom and introduce her. My mom was pregnant again. Even today, I remember that I was embarrassed to introduce her. We would never invite school friends to our home either. I would spend days and nights at their homes. When one of our children said this about our house, I hoped and was glad my Mom did not know how I felt. I felt I deserved it. I know my mother did the best she could. She had so many responsibilities and none or few tools to do anything else. We will have many conversations and joyful times when I meet her in Heaven. Since I left Kentucky, I married, and had a few times of vacation to visit afterwards. We will not allow anyone to talk bad about our Mom or what she didn't do. Again, I ask my Mom and the Lord to forgive me. "Honor your Father and your Mother." Exodus 20:12.

After Dad and Mom died, Charlie, my brother bought the old house at auction. He lived in Indy and it was inconvenient, so he sold the house to our baby brother, Tommy. He had two girls and neither of them wanted to live there, because of distance and 20 acres overgrown.

We walked to school and the kids made fun of us and hit us. My dear mother went to the parents of those that were hitting us and then the bullying ceased. They started making fun of clothes they had given us, but I was determined to get a high school diploma so the bullying was like water from the ducks back. "Only truth can dispel the words the bullies use toward you, not eye service of the flesh, men pleasers, but of sincerity of heart, fearing God in Colossians 3:22. And this is what He says about LOVE in 1 John 4:19. "We love Him because He first loved us." I don't know if the parents spanked their children. It was not talked about but it was not happening any more. The Bible was never involved.

When we got out of line, I only remember one time, it was after school when I was in 6th or7th grade.

Part 1

I was changing my school clothes and I returned practically nude, my mom asked a couple of us to go and get wood for the stove. I hummed and hawed and finally she had had enough. She did not need a switch. Her hand was sufficient, and she did a good job.

I don't ever remember being hugged or told that I was loved. The minister shook hands with our parents after the sermon; this was the closest to a symbol of love. We exited and sadly, we applied the same teachings as our parents. So glad the Lord showed me real love.

I wanted to go to college and get a secretarial six-month certificate. But there was no money or grants. So, on my next birthday, I married a truck driver and got a job in a Rexall drug store. We traveled in the southern states and had our first child a year later in Bowling Green, Kentucky. We were always moving to keep with the city he was hauling from. The first time was Indianapolis, Indiana we were in a trailer court for the first time. Our second son or third because I lost a child that (the Lord told me later that it was a girl and would have been (twins) was born in Franklin, Ky. His milk went right through him; we had to put him on soybean milk.

A Mother's Grief

I had child number four and I had no car, had never been to the doctor, snow up to my knees, and no food in the house.

My brother, Charlie, kept a watch on me. I fell going to the store for bread. Thank the Lord, no harm. I went into labor two nights later. My brother took me to all the hospitals, but no one would take me because I had no insurance. The General Hospital took me and the baby was born immediately. I went into a seizure, but the doctor said it was stress. They let me go in a couple days but not my daughter. She had jaundice, so they had to check with some doctor in New York. That night my husband took us to the Drive-Inn, and when my milk came in, I cried all night wanting my baby. The next day I got her and the doctor said to have her blood tested frequently,

The second time I lived in Indianapolis, the same trailer park, I guess I had outstayed my welcome, because, the owners came to see me and said we were three months behind in the rent

They wanted me to go to court to tell where my husband was so they could to get their money. I agreed so they would not put us out. Little did I know, they could not put us out because, I had children and it was in winter. At midnight my husband

Part I

came and said I will take you home, and then we will move to Ohio.

I was expecting baby number five and he was born in Bowling Green, Ky. In September of that year I was ironing when I knew in my heart my marriage was over and ended. The Lord had spoken. My husband was a bum and never paid his bills. He used people men and women for his own benefit and was a whoremonger.

I began to prepare to make plans to take care of my children. I got my high school books and looked at short hand and secretarial necessities. I asked my parents if they would take care of my children after I gave birth to my son.

I had two brothers in Indianapolis that I could stay with and a first cousin that owned a Drive-In Restaurant, I had a place and a job. Since there were only food handling positions, I knew I needed more education. I enrolled in the Indiana Technical Institute for a six- month course in Secretarial Training. Then the Employment office in Indianapolis got me a job as a Receptionist at REMC (running Electric lines to farmland).

Meanwhile, I had started dating. I did not know where husband was and he was Not paying child

A Mother's Grief

support. I got a call from the court house in Bowling Green, Ky asking me if he was paying support and I told them he was not. The Sheriff asked if I would come down and go before the Supreme Court to make sure he did pay. Then I had a visit, of course, and he wanted to get back together. I made it clear and he left the next day.

I had been to the Welfare Office since they could not find my husband and make Him pay support. So, I asked for them to pay my child care while I worked. Finally, they did and I gave it to my sister, Janet, who was eighteen and came to live with me and take care of my children. I was a happy camper because I had my children with me.

My boyfriend I had been dating for a few months was building a home and took me to see this magnificent home that was almost done. One only would image what was going through my mind, however we had not discussed marriage. The next Monday I received a letter in the mail saying, he was a married man. I was devasted. One wonderful thing that I thank him for was going to get my children that I had left with my mother, because I didn't have a car. Then I discovered I was expecting. Then, the company I worked for fired me and sent me on my way

Part I

with a new washer. All of those in the company were Christians (so they said). I often think of many times we feel everything will be okay by giving gifts, we can overlook our sin. I did need a Washer. For the Lord looks upon the heart, according to 2 Samuel 16:7 "But the Lord said to Samuel, look not on his countenance, or on the height of his stature; because I have refused Him, for the Lord seeth, not as man seeth; for man looketh on the outward appearance, but The Lord looketh on the heart."

If we look closely, after tribulations, the Lord has given us many blessings, I only realized yesterday of the good in life that happened fifty years ago. I choose to thank him for it today. Because it made a great difference.

What was I going do? How was I going to feed the children? No business would hire a pregnant woman, and women were classified as prostitutes or tramps if she had a child out of wedlock. There was no other way except taking quinine which killed females before the ambulance got them to the hospital. Also, if you wanted to give your child away after birth there were homes for unwed mothers run by the Catholics. However, one would have to be a Catholic. I remember that I wanted to do a term paper on priests and mother said NO because they were not hospitable or friendly. I found in the Bible where if you had sex before marriage it was a sin of adultery (Exodus 20:14) Lord forgive me and Hebrews 10:17 says and their sins and inquities will I remember no more. If I was born in today society, I would have considered abortion because I did not know it was murder but It may not have made any difference because I was not even thinking about the Lord. Dear Sweet One, if this is your plight, Jeremiah 1:5: says "Before I formed you in the womb, I knew you; before you were born I sanctified you." Jesus knew you before you would go through this so He gave you this verse 1 John 1:9 to get you back on track. It says, if we confess our sins. He Is faithful and just to forgive us our sins and to cleanse us from all unrighteousness.

This young lady that was born to us is such a blessing and we are so glad to have her. She loves the Lord, honors her parents, with much respect.

After my discovery, my brother had a friend that was seeing another lady and had been to the house several times. This time he came to the house to show me his new car. It was Really black and beautiful. Out of the blue, he said he cared about me and he had left his Friend. I said, "well you probably don't

Part I

want me since I am with child." He said that when he said he loved me, that meant the children. We rented a house and lived together. I quit my job, and became a house wife.

In 1969, being fed up with in-fighting with the relatives and a city that did not have room or children, we selected Oregon as our home for a fresh start. A past girlfriend called and said she was coming to kill me. Before we left Indy, we stopped child support after two checks and welfare for child care. We rented a house on Stark Street, in front of a Baptist Church in October that year we asked about getting married with us two, minister, my sister, and secretary. Little did my husband know he would be back where he was when in service, he came to Oregon.

We lived on the South East Side of town for two years before we rented a small 3 Bedroom house in Aloha. Six months later our landlord's older home came up for sale. Since it was an older three story, home, we felt it would be large enough to raise our seven children. Nineteen years later our big three story, house went on the market since it was time to get a smaller home. Then It was time to change the children's last name. We had already stopped the custody money so only needed to change their last name. There was a lawyer in our church who took care of this. My husband was a drinker and I never thought about it, since no one drank in our household. Dad drank a couple of beers once, fell all over the place, but we laughed. He only chewed tobacco, and mother told him to stop spitting on the stove. As time went on it became more and more with my husband. He was working two jobs and this was his only relief. But most people are not the same after drinking.

We girls, my sister and two of our daughters were spending time together and my Daughters told me that their Dad was touching them. When we got home, I talked about it, and I said this was wrong and no more. After we went to bed, I checked the girls and all appeared okay. I was really mad and I knew what the Bible says according to Matthew 18:6, but whoever Causes one of these little ones who believe in Me to sin, it would be better for him if a milestone Were hung around his neck, and he were drowned in the depth of the sea." It also refers to any new believer.

Of course, there were many promises that it would not happen again. As the days went by, I was not comfortable and really concerned. I suggested a separation and he would go and get help. We also asked the girls if they wanted to go to one of the sessions. They did not want to go. He went to the church for help from the minister. It is really hard to know and trust of any addiction for others. So, I went at times and was really shamed but I needed to know and how to help. We were separated for months. He asked the girls to forgive him and also me. Praise the Lord, and he has gotten closer to the Lord. He cannot speak about the Lord without weeping, since the Holy Spirit came into his life. After Jesus, he is my love.

After going through this sex problem, I wondered why there is no help places for men. Are they to be quiet with shame since there is shelter and help on every corner, for women? Forgot It's a women world. However, if not a Christian, where would they go? Is there any help for men? If they were abused as children?

Another story of a near death when Jesus sent a Samaritan. The earliest time I remember was when I was in Kindergarten and standing in the winter waiting for the school bus, with my sister and brother. We had, obviously, missed the bus because a car stopped and picked us up and took us home. I don't remember if they told us if we had missed the bus. We were near frozen.

A Mother's Grief

Another time I came home from school with this girl called Patsy. She was in my class. I must have been jealous of her, and I was doing all these antics, I fell and hurt myself, but I embarrassed. How prideful.

I am a loner, what can I say. I think the Lord made me this way. My older sister was two years older and was my best friend. We would go into the woods and tell each other all that happened at School or romance of other friends and dirty jokes which was he kissed her. We also had to carry water from the spring, about one- half mile, I would refuse to carry my pail, and she would carry both. So sorry Hallie. And when we fought, I would pull her hair because she was tender headed, so I always won. She never told Mother on me. She worked in the cafeteria at school and would bring food out to me, since I was too prideful to be a worker and no money to eat in the cafeteria. All good thing comes to an end. It was our responsibility to wash the dishes, after dinner. As usual She always had to go to the toilet which took a century.

Our friendship came to an end. When My dear sister met a man and started dating which did not please me because I had to go with her. This was the guy she married at sixteen. The family was going to break up and my mom was raising her voice. Hallie was stomping her feet, and I was crying because my sister was going to leave us. This had never happened before. At the end of our friendship, I became a loner, knowing to depend on Barbara, even if today, I never meet a stranger. I compare myself to wine, the older I get the better I get the more I love Jesus. Remember, in the years that I was born and raised; children were to be seen and not heard. Therefore, there was no talking. There was no complaining; we needed to be responsible without any excuses, because we were all in the same boat and no asking for help. You did the best you could and it was accepted. We were all trying to exist and survive another day, especially in the country If you were not wealthy. Many times there were no transportation, so we walked. We walked half mile to a teacher's house to get a ride to Sunday school. Also, most times the father or Man, of the house ruled at least until we moms woke up or we trusted what was right and what was wrong. My Mom got some money from relatives who had died. Then she bought a Model A, Ford, got her license, and learned to drive. My Dad would not ride with her because he was fearful of cars and planes. I think it is all learning about each other and how to work together.

A Mother's Grief

The scripture that I think and is my foundation so many times is in Philippians 4:13 "I can do All things through Christ who strengthens me."

Most husbands and wives are opposites so we are no different. I am the loner, and hubby does not like to be alone. Also, he rarely drinks, beer now and then, and stopped smoking when his grandson said it was not good for him.

In 1972 I went to work for Tektronix as an order entry clerk for $1.97 @ hour. After 18 ½ years at Tektronix Field Administration I worked as a Contract Administration for the Federal Government 3-4 more years. I quit Tektronix in 1992 and took temporary jobs when got bored.

As I am thinking of my heritage, I want to share the first time when I really experienced sadness. We lived in Oakland, Kentucky in a hotel that had been turned into housing. It was very close to the railroad track that stopped outside out our front door. It stopped every day to give mail to post office. We kids was always waiting when it stopped, because people on the train threw out money. This had been going on for a long time since we found lots of coins farther down the hill. My sister and I dug up many coins and when we went to bed that night, Hallie said if

Part I

she died during the night, she wanted me to have her coins. She did not die, but our brother died the next morning. A new born brother died with mucus and could not breathe.

Until mother had baby Dale, my older sister and I did the cooking. I remember I spilled grease on my leg, but I was okay next day. It sure hurt. Mother let us all hold the baby after He was born so she knew something was wrong. He had so much mucus, so took him to hospital. Dad went to a neighbor to call the hospital to check on baby. The next day, I looked down railroad track and saw him coming home. His head was bending low and I knew baby Dale was dead. Then I knew my sister was seeing a death but not hers but our brother.

My dad's mother (grandma) was with us at this time, and I was sick and had been in bed for a while. She came and asked what could she do or what did I want, and I said milk. She walked across the street and purchased a quart of milk. I drank it immediately, then in the morning I was much better and back to my old self. Again, the Lord sufficed more than enough.

If you will permit me to share with you about my walk with the Lord, it would be a Blessing For me

A Mother's Grief

and hopefully for you. As I said earlier that my parents were Christians, however. It does not make me a Christian nor is it inherited. Each of us need to know that we need to say yes to a Savior. Jesus died for our sins and we are telling Him we want Him to be a part of our lives in all ways. We want Him to forgive us for our sins. As my great granddaughter said at Christmas when she was talking about Jesus having a thorn crown put on His head before being crucified. She was crying after her reading in the Bible that I bought her when she was four years old. Matthew 27:29 "When they had twisted a crown of thorn, they put it on His head, and a reed in His right hand. And they bowed the knee before Him and mocked Him, saying, "Hail King of the Jews!' Then after accepting Jesus, one needs to be baptized for a necessity for entering the Kingdom of heaven. Matthew 3:15 "But Jesus answered and said to Him. Permit it to be so. Now, for thus it is fitting for us to fulfill all righteousness." Also, there is a scripture in John 3:5 saying, "Jesus answered and said to him. Most assuredly, I say to you, unless one is born of water and the Spirit, he cannot enter the Kingdom of God." The water is the Baptism, which should follow one's acceptance of Jesus.

Part I

We are living in a world that the Bible and others (who love people) want to share the joy that we have and peace. When I was growing up there was no talking about Jesus, even in church. Most of the time Christians responded at the Altar Call. They were older people asking teenagers if they wanted to pray at the altar. Since we were respectable to older folks, we went forth without knowing why and waited for it to be over. Today I find there is always an opportunity to find the word and others find Jesus much easier. The question is, yes or no and hopefully they have been told of Jesus as our Savior. The Lord will always open the door.

As you read my story, you will know I have made wrong decisions and sinned during the 78 years I have existed. Many things have taken my time and energy even though I was a church goer for many years. Praise the Lord, for He knew I was a slow learner.

I was in my early fifties before I got serious with my walk with the Lord. I started reading the Bible every day when our pastor asked the congregation to sign up to read the Bible for Easter. He wanted us to be praying and reading 24/7 until Easter.

I continued after Easter, and I got up an hour before work so I would have time to read the Bible before I left. I got involved in a Bible Study, led a Bible Study, led a prayer chain, and volunteered for many other opportunities in the church. I do know that I am a servant and will always be a helper because I love people. I read many Christian books and seek any that will help me to know the Lord any way that will bring me closer to my Savior.

PART 2

Death

ON A BLUSTERY dark Sunday evening on November 2, 1991 I received the worse news a parent could ever hear. The grand kids were playing and waiting because everyone was hungry after coming from church. I remember it was an evening of peace until at about 7:30 when we answered the door. Two detectives asked us to please remove our three grandchildren to another room. Detectives, Sue Hill and Bob Norman proceeded to tell us that our daughter had been killed and that was as much as they knew at that time.

Of course, we wanted to question them if they were sure but they already knew and prepared to tell us the story.

My daughter was born September 4, 1961 in

A Mother's Grief

Orlando, Florida in the Seventh Adventist Hospital. It was a smooth birth, except that I missed my coffee after birth. It is not allowed according to their religion. I think they called it Sanka because it has no caffeine. After we got home, I let her sleep with me because she was breast fed, her until and the thunders and lightings would come out of nowhere waking her. I continued to breast feed her until my milk was not nourishing enough to sustain for growth. Doctor said she was too small for her age. I think she was fearful of lightning and thunder most of her life.

Belinda was a really good baby. Even growing up, there were never problems or Issues with clothes. Her younger sister was not allowed to wear her clothes. This sister was the opposite of her and threw her clothes on the floor or under the bed. Belinda hung her clothes up and she was a perfectionist. Guess who was working in the yard on Saturday and playing ball with the boys and who was in the house picking out her clothes for the next day? However, they were close and even lived together for a while. The younger would defend the older. Their fights were only at home.

Belinda was not rebellious, talkative, or loud but quiet. Looking back, she was a Listener and was

PART 2

absorbing, patiently, probably more than was needed before knowing or understanding consequences.

When she was in the first grade we went to Wichita, Kansas for a new job. The school said she was failing, slow, and needed more instruction before the end of school. Then we were laid off for months and returned to Indianapolis, Indiana. We had gone to Kansas because of a friend's advice that we had spent a lot of time with when we lived in Indianapolis. Friends kept our children while we were working

My husband worked for, Cessna, an airplane company which was a lot like Tektronix. It was friendly, laid back, and easy going. When he was laid off, none of the airplane Companies compared to Cessna, and he lost his heart to continue in that line of work,

There were two interesting things about Wichita. It was a dry county and the bars had only beer. Everyone brought tomato juice to give the beer a flavor, and the entertainment was dancing fat ladies, 500-600 pounds in weight.

After much discussion and traveling from place to place, we decided to make our home In Oregon. My husband had lived in Oregon and he loved it. We had family problems, revenge from friendships, and the schools were on strike in Indy, In. Never last but

A Mother's Grief

first we felt a divine calling. Here we are in Oregon and home.

On our way we discovered our funds was depleted, and I was sick because our last child was only six months old. The doctor did not know what was wrong or where the blood was coming from, but I got better. I felt I had a tubal and was miscarried. We stopped and rented a house in Salt Lake City, in Utah. We asked my sister, Janet, if she would look after the children while my husband and I went on to Oregon to find work.

As I look back, this was the second time that I asked her to care for our children. She was only in her early twenties. Thank you, dear sister Janet, and you remember this, I know. My children love you with all their hearts and so do I. You cooked for them when there were very little food in the house. They loved biscuits and gravy and you did not complain, and it was delicious. I will always love you to the end of time.

I was eight years older than Janet and I loved to dress her up when she was a toddler. Janet was a beauty, with strawberry blonde (close to red) hair. After a couple of years in Oregon, Janet went home to Kentucky and married a minister's son. I will always

PART 2

miss her, even though we talk frequently. We are sisters, friends, and loved ones.

It was strawberry picking time in Oregon, but there was no need for any more pickers. Jobs were scarce. My husband even went to Red Cross to get enough money to go back and get our children in Utah, but they said no. My hubby was a welder. A truck company in Durham gave him a job and advanced money to us to go back and get our children. They did not know but the Lord did, and we repaid them with great joy. Thank you, Lord.

After we came to Oregon and settled in, we found that the schools taught differently than Kansas, and Belinda fit well into the new school system. The Lord will bring many events and thoughts into our lives. It is no mistake but was intended, "Praise His Name."

We had made a wonderful decision to move to Oregon from Indianapolis, Indiana. We brought just what would fit in a small Plymouth with seven children and my sister. We stopped for coffee then continued on but disagreed about something. We didn't watch the road nor realize we were on the brink of the Colombia, River. I cry as I tell this story, because all ten of us would have drowned if Jesus had not lifted us to higher ground. "When you pass through the waters, I will be with you and through the rivers they shall not overflow you. When you walk through the fire you shall not be burned, nor shall the flame scorch you." Isaiah 43:2

We found a two- room building in a trailer park on Stark Street for a while. Then We bought a small house in Multnomah County. After we paid for it and began to build We were told we did not have enough land. After the strawberry season, we rented a new house in Aloha. We had wonderful neighbors. I told my husband that the children Needed to be in church, and, I was promised it would happen just as soon as we got moved into a house. The promise had been kept.

Then all of us started going to church. The children loved to go to camp and my husband loved Bible reading after dinner. The older children accepted the Lord and were Baptized. There were lots of outings in Sunday School and friends, gathering from house to house. I was reading Bible stories to the little ones in Sunday School.

When Belinda, that was behind in Kansas, went into third grade in Oregon we had no more problems in school. We never discovered what the earlier problem was, but we were very thankful. Maybe

PART 2

it was because we were more settled than before or maybe school system was different. Here is a letter from Church Camp.

One of the letters we received in June 26. 1974 from camp saying:

Dear Mom & Dad,

I really miss you a lot. The first day we got up at 4:15. It took us about 6 hours to get here and we had to register And we wanted to swim but the swimming period was over. We are really having a good time there is a lot of cute Boys here. I am meeting a lot of friends. We went on a hike Today and we got wet. Love

Every Mother's Day, birthday, and Christmas I received gifts from her such as pictures, Jewel, and paintings. Belinda loved me and always took my side. When my mother tried to keep her while I ran an errand, she fought until I returned even though she was only two and half years old and had been around her grandma countless times. She was a fighter. Belinda let her twins visit her other grandma but when she when to get them for Christmas, this Grandma said she let them go somewhere else. Belinda said, "if I don't have my children this evening I will return with the police." The grandma tried to restrain her and Belinda picked up the coffee table and threw it at her. They were with us at Christmas. Thanks Lord.

A Belated Birthday Wish (no date)
I love you very much, you'll always be my best friend. Thanks for all your love, support and help. PS. Your looking better than ever before.
From Belinda

We did not allow any car dates until our girls were, sixteen years old. Shortly after this age, Belinda and sister went to parties with friends. We also allowed dances which were every Saturday because they chaperoned and they were home at a decent hour.

In March Belinda called me at work and asked and if she could have lunch with me and talk. She was getting close to completing the 11th grade. She told me she was pregnant, that evening we called the boy and asked him what was he going to do about the baby, and he said he would give her the money for an abortion. We said no and we would take care of the baby if he did not to want to care of him or her. Robert was born in December. I fell in love right

PART 2

away. We already had a grandson, and they were with us most of the time. We also had two girls in high school. But I never worried about what I didn't have, nor any dreams of stardom.

Since my husband and I worked five days a week, we needed a baby sitter. Then we found Belinda could not go back to school and finish because she had too many credits lacking for graduation. Then she got a job and took the baby to a sitter. Next Belinda decided to move in with a friend so she and the baby moved. I received a message from friend that the baby had been left and needed changing. We went and got our grandson.

Belinda took care after school, but it is different when it is your own. It's a responsibly, that never leaves you. Our grandson was with us a lot, but there was, times when we didn't know where he was. We worried and prayed for protection and no harm, until kindergarten. I would use my lunch time to take him to school and back home. One year he had missed 35 days. Praise the Lord, we began to take him to church and we had seen great joy and honesty from this young man. He knows Jesus, and his trials may be the reason it happened.

Some where in between, Belinda got a boy friend

and they were together for a while. He was an addict, and stayed home. Robert answered the door one day and the boyfriend whipped him with an electric cord. Sometimes we suspected Belinda was using drugs, but it was never obvious, when we were together.

In 1986 we were watching TV and the news came on about a fire in Portland at an apartment saying the names of our grandchildren. Thank goodness the Lord had spared them, the older grandson was the baby sitter. Many days later he came to me and told Me what he had done and the price he paid to take care of his little sister, since he was only seven. I told him it was not his fault and we prayed and asked the Lord's forgiveness. There was much guilt but a wonderful freedom. When I look back, I question how he did know that this was a sin. Also, it was revealed that the boyfriend set the fire to get money from the Red Cross.

My sweet daughter did not know what she wanted and was searching with the wrong crowd. We talked with her regarding the crowd she was running with. She said it is such a rush. She knew some people that was doing the same but got off the streets and they told her also. We would not allow her to bring her friends to our house because of the children.

PART 2

One time she did not have a place to live so we let her stay in our guest house until she made other arrangements, but I came the next afternoon and there was a stranger. I walked over and said you are not welcome here now or ever or again, I reminded Belinda of the promise we made and when and when we set rules. She decided to leave and was gone the next day, without a goodbye.

Belinda worked for Fred Meyer, hair Salon, dancer, was model, but she was never satisfied. Her twins spent a lot of time with their other grandma. She was thinking about getting married and we were so happy. But after all the preparations there was a no show.

One other time she was seeing a very nice- looking guy that loved her children, even though the twins were climbing all over him. We did not know him and he could have been mean to her. However, we had high hopes for some maturity.

My husband and I were coaching when the children were in grade school and the Grandchildren would always try to find their parents in the crowd. We enjoyed the time with the children even though we were working 40 hours each week and sometimes over time. We sure were glad for hot dogs. Many nights that was dinner after the games. Actually, one

A Mother's Grief

of our daughters liked hot dogs better than steak. No problem! Also, I joined PTA to help out in many ways. I remember at one meeting I found a book in the library that had no clothes on the characters. I am sure it would be acceptable today. However, it was removed.

The last time I saw my daughter alive was the previous week before she was killed. She came by in the evening to bring some new shoes for one of the twins. I remember standing on the porch waving good-bye as long as I could see her. In November 2006 I wrote:

"THE MYSTERY DEATH OF DECTIVE SUSAN HILL"

Who is Susan Hill and what has she got to do with my daughter? I will never forget her Because of the grave image she portrays on my mind. It was this month many years ago that we met. It was a Sunday night. She and Bob Norman (detectives) knocked on our door and asked if they could come in and talk with us.

I was not suspicious even though they had identified themselves as detectives. They also asked if we take the grandchildren to another room. Even when she identified their mission, it was unbelievable and

PART 2

I am sure it was not Belinda. I asked if she was sure that the person that was murdered was our daughter and she said she was sure. She had already been positively identified.

So began our few short years with Susan Hill, trying to solve the case of who had killed our daughter. Since I had a dream the previous evening and remembered the name that the Lord gave me. Fortunately, there was a person by that name that was involved with Belinda. I had never seen or heard Belinda talk about this person.

Susan pursued many avenues but could not find or get enough evidence to charge him or detain him for any length of time. They charged him with parole violation and kept him in jail hoping he would divulge or talk to another convict about the murder. She also increased the reward if anyone would come forward with information. However, all of this was to no avail.

Bob and Susan were very good for us. We learned that her husband was also in law enforcement and her thanksgiving would be a working day like any other. They went to an ex boyfriends house and retrieved all of our daughter's possessions and brought them to our house. (Even after all these years I cry

A Mother's Grief

for her son, who was twelve years old, and crying as relatives take her dresses and possessions).

We were very saddened when Susan was killed July 17, 1996 in an airplane crash on a long, awaited vacation to France on TWA Flight 800. I hope she did not suffer. This is how we know Mrs. Susan Hill. The last time saw her alive was at the Billy Graham Crusade in1993 in downtown Portland. The cause of the crash was determined to be the fuel in an almost empty tank vaporized in an explosion. Every one who knew her solely misses her. So, this tribute of Susan will be added to Belinda's Scrapbook. Always remember her and wonder why she died at this time.

PART 3

Before & After

NOW IT IS time to bury her. We gathered at the graveside for services in Valley Memorial Park on November 5, 1991. The funeral home dressed her in her Younger Sister's dress which was so beautiful. Her children viewed their Mom the day before services. It was a somber day. The twins cried when we went home and we could not comfort them. Do not know how we got through it? Of course, today I know how we all survived.

The service was full of loved ones and family. Some of the friends wanted the casket to be opened because they had not seen her. I remember the twins were Holding on to me. The detectives were there also.

LOVE

SAINT FRANCIS

Make me an instrument of your peace where there is hatred, let me show love Where there is injury, pardon, where-there is doubt, faith, where there is, despair, hope, where there is darkness light, and where there is sadness joy

O, Divine Master, grant that I may not so much seek to be consoled as to console, to be understood as to understand, to be loved as to love, for it is in giving that we receive, it is in pardoning that we are pardoned, and it is in dying That we are born to eternal life.

We had the children until the end of the that school term. However, it was not what the other Grandma wanted. She said we need to go to court and we did, but the Dad said he wanted them to stay with the Flannigans. This was done until end of school.

As expected, the grandmother came back to claim them and we went to court a second time. The court gave them to the grandmother. The grandmother did

PART 3

not come to court. She only replied via the phone. When the Twin boy was getting his belongings he said "Grandma don't worry; it's 'only for vacation. But, I saw the writing on the wall. I continued to call and kept in touch, every time asking if we could see them, or have them for vacation. She did let us sometimes but the last time when he was fourteen and she sent him to Alaska. The girl did not want to leave grandma because she was princess and favored (just like Jacob).

Belinda's older son Robert (12 years old) was wanting to go to his Dad's in California before the new the school started. So, we sent him, with the money from the death of his Mother. I cried not knowing if I would ever see him again. These kids sure have been on a journey.

I got a letter from the District Attorney of Multnomah County to let us know when the trial was to begin in October of this year. We got the letter May 3, 2005.

PART 4

Burial

JURY SELECTION WAS to be this week and next/ trial 17th through 19th in Portland, Oregon. We were hoping trial will be starting in October this year. Our team consisted of Deputy DA, Lawyer, and an advocate. They were the best and we felt very comfortable.

Belinda had been shot in the head and her blood was under the sink. She was found the next morning when someone saw her door open. There was rumor of a drug deal gone wrong. Others reasons were rejection, and money. Word was that there was a safety box? Mostly the reason for this killing was jealously. Corner said she had been moved according to her liver. Stiff as a board, and had been there 12 hours. The expected trial was to last six weeks.

Plan-A was aggravated murder which carried a

second penalty, for guilt or innocence or appropriate punishment deliberative, or intentional (execute)-yes. Plan B, carries dangerous/threat to society-yes. Should death penalty be imposed, life in prison with parole, after thirty years or death? The law in 1991, (a) Death, (b) Life in prison without parole (c) thirty years but parole at twenty years, mandatory life sentence/option of parole in 20 years with evidence of rehabilitation. One criminalist said, "Lord, Belinda's blood cries out to you for justice." Genesis 4:10. There was a trace of drug in her system and her purse was never found.

I don't know if this is any benefit to others, however it was given to us and was for jurors and ourselves. Honestly, it was in my notes and at that time, we were so emotional it did not sink in. We pray that it would be a blessing to others.

We had six women and six men jurors, but when it came time to decide punishment an alternate was chosen because of sickness. The verdict was death by the jurors. Multnomah County Circuit Court jury deliberated six hours for two hours for two days to reach the verdict. We went back to court December 5, 2005 for the hearing in which the judge formally imposed the death penalty on the murderer.

The last death row person in Multnomah County Circuit Court was handed down in 2000, was Eric Runner.

After the verdict, all of the jurors came to see us to get acquainted. They wanted to know how the twins were and how was life, going to be with us. We were so moved and felt loved. And we were; He was with us.

I had no idea what went on in a trail. Believe or not, there was a fire drill. The witnesses were in the car when she was shot, and they knew what had happened because the murderer told many people as he steamed about what she had done to him.

Most of the guys were together this night because they were all basketball players at the college. One witness lied to the police when he was questioned and went to Finland from fear but returned to tell the truth. Before he left, we got to speak with him and thanked him for His honesty. He had married and had one child. One other witness was so angry we were expecting him to grab the murderer right there and kill him. More police were called until witness finished. Evidence was so long coming because the murderer was in jail for 60 months on a drug conviction during that time. The murderer could not keep his month shut while he bragged to several inmates. The result was admission of murder in the late 1990's. Then an indictment by the prosecutor in 2002. Davis had an extensive record of arrests and convictions starting when he was age 9.

In 1998 Ronald Teal in the Oregon State Penitentiary has died since, but he got Davis to give up details of the murder. We got to see him on the video. He didn't have long to live. I believe it was cancer. We were so thankful for him and prayed that he did not suffer.

There were five more people Davis met in prison who testified that he had confessed as recently as late July. The trail started in October.

It seems we will never be free of constant appeals, even if he is incarcerated for the rest of his life. We learned at the last appeal, that when he uses all the appeals here, he can go federal. We are reminded with each appeal that he needs some attention, and we will live all of the previous grief again. Some how I do not see this as punishment for him, but more grief for us. In December 2018 I surrendered Davis to my Savior. Jesus created him and He has a plan for Davis. Hallelujah, I am free. All these appeals were in Salem, Oregon.

Appeal 1-was to determine if our lawyer had made an error – which was not

Appeal 2 – trial because IQ was less than 79; can't be on death row

His family was notified to tell how atrocious and in human treatment by family Members. So, I put in my two cents as below:

> I do not think or believe your status in the prison system should change Loved ones and the prisoners will not be safe, otherwise. After all, that is why, the jury put you on death row, so that everyone would be safe in prison.
>
> It is enough, to be reminded every time we think of you and the injury and grief we feel and experience. Belinda's children search for mementoes to remember their mother as the years pass. With all the wrong you have done how can you ask to be among other people? Everyone's safety will be comprised.
>
> For you have taken something that was not yours and could never replace. Shame on you! I dare say, there have not been any changes for the good in you as a person since you were incarcerated in 2005. Why do you feel you deserve a change in your status?

Part 4

I seek to leave you with a Scripture that applies to us all. Do not be deceived God will not be mocked: whatsoever a man sows that he will also reap. So why do you deserve anything else but death or do you believe you deserve better than death. Is this what you have sown? Did you give Belinda a choice, so to be fair, you should not have a choice? Oh, by the way, this is Scripture, but also a promise.

The people spoke in 2005 and we should continue to abide by their decision.

So, he was taken off death row and was to spend his life in prison without parole. The next appeal was last December 2018; we heard a lawyer which brought up that the Coroner didn't properly or calculate the hours since last meal; have not received an answer. Romans 13:3-4 specifically talks baring the sword for capital punishment. (3) For rulers are not a terror to good works, but to evil. Do you want to be unafraid of the authority? Do what is good, and you will have praise from the same. (4) For he is God's minister to you for good. But if you do evil, be afraid: for he does not bear the sword in vain: for he is God's minister, an avenger to execute wrath on him who practices evil. Some people call Romans the government book of the Bible.

My thoughts: Oregon needs to make sure a fairness is given to those who have been hurt by their acts on society. Such as appeals, but it is okay for them to not show up. Make it more difficult for them rather, than to just ring a bell. We already pay everything for them. We should get a tax deduction.

PART 5

Trial & Penalties

AS I LAY my pen down, one more thought contains grief when it first happened and twenty-eight years later. The pain of losing a child will always be remembered and a part of that pain will always be there.

However, you will always be sensitive to others pain, because you have been there. Even when it is a story on TV.

When I wrote this many years ago, I said that faith in a supreme being was very Important, which is true, but today I say: "Why Do I Love Jesus."

Because He was faithful and watched over me when I turned from Him as a teenager, but He heard my voice and my supplications and has inclined His ear to me as Psalm 11:1 says: In the Lord I put my trust; How can you say to my soul, flee as a bird, to your

A Mother's Grief

mountain? He has been with me during all my trials and He has borne my grief. He is the only One that can give me peace from worry, anxiety, past mistakes, and has forgiven me for all my sins. Thank you, Sweet Jesus. He loved me first and because He died on the cross to save me from my sins. While I was still a sinner, He died for me. Thou has done great things for me and wonderous things. Psalm 73: says Whom have I in heaven but you? And there is none upon earth that I desire beside thee. One more in Psalm 116:1-2, I love the Lord, because He has heard my voice and my supplications (2) Because He has inclined His ear to me. Therefore, I will call upon Him as long as I live. I have learned Jesus will pursue me and He has compassion for which is one of His characteristics. For I have to go to Him frequently for He is always there like now telling you about the loss of my two boys.

Darrell was killed in a motor cycle accident. He loved to speed down the road. He was a quiet young man, was always loved his family, and great handyman. Loved to eat and was patient. He died in 1982, leaving a wife and two children. Was going home when it happened and was not discovered until the next day.

The coroner knocked, in the early morning when

he told us. I immediately looked in his bedroom and saw he was not there, but I had to see him to make sure. I did, kissed his face in the funeral home and reality set in. My first thought was I had not said good-by the previous day.

Darrell was our second child, only 22 years old, was a Christian and had been baptized. Loved his son and daughter. His son was 2-3 years old and was walking around his dad's casket, in the grass, which I thought, would he ever remember this. He is our first grandchild. Belinda threw a rose in his casket, not knowing she would be next to die.

Then Danny was our fifth child. Was good in school and needed lots of attention. He could excel at practically anything. We have pictures that show him receiving certificates for Bible study. There were no problems, until teenage years.

Then everything he did was to get attention. Started drinking and we begged him to go for help and he did for a few days but left on his own. Don't think we heard of by- polar. Danny loved his mother, was always bringing flowers, and planted them in my yard. He told me it felt like the devil was on one shoulder and the Lord was on the other shoulder. We told him that the devil will not win.

A Mother's Grief

Two days before his death we talked. We had time together, hugging and praying, and talking. Was very concerned about him and at end of prayer, I wept He said "I made my Mom cry." At the end, He put himself in harms way. Danny, had a heart of gold. Died when he was 38 years and left a wife and four children. I shall hope some way this is a blessing to others, which is my desire.

> We cannot know what lies ahead
> From day to passing day.
> What changes God is planning
> In his wise and loving way.
> We cannot know the reasons
> He allows both joy and tears.
> Why we must lose the precious ones
> We've cherished through the years.
> We cannot know—but we can trust,
> And faith can help us find
> Our way to those tomorrows
> That will bring us peace of mind.

However, I cried, and cried, and cried and since I am a reader and was born in the silent years I am late with, speak your mind. I begin to put my words on paper, to express my grief and to find truth within myself, and reflect again and again. May I share with a Broken Heart? If not, you may skip!

PART 6

Hope

GRIEF IS THE price you pay for the ability to love; you think you will stop hurting. The dictionary defines grief as a deep sadness caused by trouble or loss, anguish, or heavy sorrow. One phrase I heard was a hole so deep in the middle of your heart that it aches and hurts. To some this is an adequate description and to others it may not be so consuming. This was my feelings when my thirty-year- old daughter died of a gun shot wound.

Let me describe the symptoms of grief. Shock and numbness inhabit the body and you move in a trance like state. Most of the circumstances surrounding your grief is unbelievable, but when a glimmer of reality tries to invade the unbelief there is so much pain that you again seek to escape. During the times of reality, you think the tears never stop, when they do one is left hoarse and weak. Weeping is supposed to be an outlet for pain but I never found it relieved the pain. Maybe crying is for those that have pent up angry. Day by day you live with this constant pain long after all the social responsibilities have been fulfilled. One wonders when you can arise and really see the sun.

One's thinking is hampered by morbidity and you feel life is useless and meaningless. Why am I still living and how will I make it? What is the reason for continuing? Which one of my loved ones will be next? Somehow, we need to find a reason and hang on until some feelings return.

Then there is that demon called guilt, that robs us of self esteem, and any positive answers. If I could only tell her how much I loved her or apologize for our disagreements. I wish I had handled things differently. Life becomes one big---IF.

Life is for the living and as long as we are a part of the human race, we must survive as such. There are loved ones left, that need you very much and if no other reason, their physical comfort and needs must be met. This is the time to draw closer and support each other in grief and love. Certainly, this is a very difficult transition but a normal routine seems to bring stability.

A Mother's Grief

Everyone grieves differently; no two people grieves alike. It is very important that you do not compare yourself to someone else. Some advice will apply and some won't. The Bible tells us that no man knows his own heart and many things we will never know About ourselves until we experience it. Like myself, I discovered that this pain of losing a child will always be remembered and a part of that pain will always be there.

Feeling is a sign that healing is taking place and as time goes on a new insight will begin to emerge. In about six months healing did begin. For instance, you will always be sensitive to others pain, because you have been there. Even when it is a sad story on TV. Be sensitive to your friends, by not always talking about your loss.

There is a lot of life to live, there is indeed life after death. Faith in a Supreme Being is very important. This belief has contributed to my sanity even though it has been three years.

A dear friend called me and gave me this scripture, which helped me. It is in Jeremiah 31: 15-16 (15) Thus says the Lord: a voice was heard in Ramah lamentation and bitter weeping, Rachel weeping for her children refusing to be comforted for her children, because they are no more. (16) Thus says the Lord, refrain your voice from weeping and your eyes from tears. For your work shall be rewarded says the Lord and they shall come back from the land of the enemy.

The End

www.ingramcontent.com/pod-product-compliance
Lightning Source LLC
Chambersburg PA
CBHW060503110426
42738CB00055B/2612